Seasons

of Grief

Seasons

of Grief

A poetry collection on healing and

finding yourself through travel

ARTI RAJPUT

Copyright

We were watching the sunset together and I asked her if she ever got bored of the sun rays pouring through the kitchen window, the blurry pastel London sunset ending in the same place every day. She answered in a blend of Hindi and English. Her words escape me, but I'll never forget how she made me feel.

So very loved.

Contents

Foreword

I hope you leave these pages feeling your load has lightened.

I've collected my poetry into three parts and you can start from whichever section you want but I've intended the following order so that the messy part, the pit, is nestled between adventure and hope.

There was a time, over a decade, where I would've refused to pick a book with *Grief* in the title, the blurb, or the marketing, because that word, to me, was admitting defeat. And that's okay because a handful of the poetry on these pages may not have been right for me back then and maybe you feel the same now. To that I say, please put this book away. It'll be here when you're ready.

I love to travel this big, beautiful world of ours and it's been healing to experience different ways of living; unbelievable landscapes, moments of thrilling adventure, and have I mentioned the challenges? Travelling is hard. Staying still is hard. And no matter what you choose to do, make sure you treat life like an adventure.

The other side to hurt isn't happiness or a life without worries. I find, the other side to hurt, pain, and loss, is living.

I hope your soul comes alive again.

Part 1

Adventure

Note:

"Catch flights not feelings." - Unknown (possible origin: 'catch feelings' - 1990s hip hop)

"Catch flights, fall in love with countries, people you've yet to meet, the food, the scenes. Catch flights, find your anchor, fall in love with yourself. Find your version of healing. Travel through grief, come back to your self. Find your peace. Catch feelings." - Arti Rajput

Travel Back to Yourself

I hope you find yourself again.
Through rainforests heavy with humidity,
through the weight of your backpack,
through the memories,
of a life well lived.

I hope you find yourself again,
that you believe,
deep diving into your life,
won't erase them.

I hope you find yourself again.

You Are Lucky

And I grin and agree
Because the way I see the world
The beauty

Aren't I? Lucky
that for me the sea winks in the sun
That nature greets me
The sun covers me in its joy

Lucky
Life is so rich and beautiful
So full and spectacular
Lucky
That I choose to see the love and beauty

Lucky
Because
I know the cost of life
Again
And
Again

The cost of life

And because I've paid

In ways you don't want to
I am forced
To see luck and opportunity
Where one might see despair

That when darkness engulfs you
The threat of not feeling undiluted joy
Is enough

Because loss on loss of loss

It numbs you-
dissolves the spark,

So when you see me
Laugh with glee
So when you hear me
talk of the future with abandon
So when you learn of my plans for the weekend, for
next month, next year
And you feel yourself riddled with
Jealousy

Just know
That I am ever so lucky
To have lost,

Even myself from time to time.

So excuse me
When I choose to love
My precious life
With an unyielding force.

Memories Are Made With You

Life is an anchor when memories are made with you,
along the weaving canalside of our youth.
Ambling along to each other's tirade,
and finding peace in the other's praise.

Life is an embrace when memories are made with you,
along the narrow cobbled pathways.
Exploring soft-sand beaches, briny mussels,
and evenings wiled away with board games.

Life is a tapestry when memories are made with you,
along the turquoise trails of coastal causeways.
Foraging markets of mouth-watering food,
and resolving to let the lightness unfold.

Life's an adventure when memories are made with you,
along the lanes of Soho, feasting on what's new.
Chasing the highs of our spontaneous travels gone by,
and chucking the rulebook to ground our minds.

Life is a fairytale when memories are made with you,
along the poolside discussing our daydreams.
Laughing until the tears run dry,
and unearthing summer flings from our uni days.

Life is a joy when memories are made with you,
along the motorways, garden days, and barbecues.
Revealing stories of sixth form escapades,
and telling you all my unfiltered truths.

Life is a treat when memories are made with you,
along the bakery queues, quick coffees, weekly meets.
Planning endless quality time as a retreat,
and brightening any bleak days with your reframes.

Life is a crescendo
when memories are made with all of you,
along the backstreets of London's brown bricks
and climbing ivy. Taking an extra minute,
or ten, to avoid the crowds,
and feel the sizzling pace of town.

The Shades of You

The red blush of yesterday,
Purple skies of tomorrow,
The yellow sun rays of today,
And the green grass of forever.
The light in your steps,
The ease in your shoulders,
With the falling of leaves,
The embrace of forever.

The flecks of gold in your irises,
When the sunshine of today
Peeks between the clouds,
The hope of forever.

The shades of you,
Forever.

Let Go (Mua Caves, Vietnam)

And in those days,
When the world feels crazed, I
close my eyes, and
come alive, with memories
of you.

The mountain dew,
The wisps of blue,
In the sky within reach.

The planks beneath my feet,
Hold me steady,
feeling my beats.

My steps carrying me on,
Unable to let go, of such
a feeling, as this,
as you.

Almost Something (Khao Sok, Thailand)

There are boats and oars,
There are oceans and rivers,
There are streams and channels,
There are silences
which lift you.

There are empty days
which trick you
Into believing there's nothing
But those oceans and rivers,
Those streams and channels.

They're forever flowing,
Life's joys trickling,
Abundance awaits in the mooring.

The Sun Sets (Pai, Thailand)

The sun sets on beautiful days
hard days, long days, tough days.

The sun sets on kind days
gentle days, exhilarating days, peaceful too.

The sun sets on our dreams of becoming
award-winning podcasters
on friendships whose pillars crack under pressure
relationships where we differ on basic human rights
worries which surface after glasses of wine
fears of repeating
our money mistakes and committing crimes

And somewhere else in the world
the sun rises.

It peaks and blooms.
Golden hour softens us
brightens lives, cultivates growth.

The sun rises despite it all.

Backpackers 1: Spontaneity

I take a deep breath

When we say goodbye.

I brush my hand against hedges,
As the water glints from fountains,
And the voices around me erupt into
laughter.

I sing lyrics into the night,
While the bassline
Thrums in the air
-borne by the crowd.

I ride through the mountains,
A thrill in my chest,
While the worries of yesterday,
Drop by the kerbside.
I sigh into my chest,
On every first night,
Of an unfamiliar city,
Fists clenched & determined.

You smile across the crowd,
As a passerby scowls,
Forging a path through,
The throngs of idlers.

You make easy conversation,
As we await our faiths, and
rejoice when we're stuck
Together; a fine choice.

You lean over the table,
Ask my opinion on pad see ew,
See me almost drool,
Finding a foodie in this hostel.
You glance away from your phone,
See me all alone,
crack a joke,
Before we know it, hours have flown.

You invite me to spend the day,
Getting lost in the valley,
amidst mountain streams and bamboo trees,
While we're chasing waterfalls.

You see my name and age,
Let it spark conversation,
So we can hike to coffee farms,
Our laughter, a relief from the heat.

You heard the way I dropped my 't',
Peppered my sentences with 'like',
And the relief flooded through you,
Here's someone to pass the time.

Because languages bring a sense of home,
Familiarity where hope can grow,
And people who were once strangers,
Become friends who never say goodbye.

Sunbathers

Sun chasers,
Sea gazers.

Chippie goers,
Fab lickers.

Tree climbers,
Picnic makers.

River walkers,
Pub goers.

Sunset watchers,
Balcony sitters.

Garden growers,
Patio grillers.

Sun chasers…

Funfair

Candy floss,
Sugar-coated fingers,

Metal clunking metal of rollercoasters,
Air heavy with piping hot doughnuts,
Determination as hard as Rock candy sticks
to live in the moment of-

Piping hot chips,
Gulls swooping for a catch.

Shrieks of delight from way up high,
Cross-country trains pulling in,
"Come one, come all",
of the games-master, telling you the

Popcorn's salted and sweet,
Escaping between handfuls,

Like the laughter through your teeth.

Spring At Home

The English Rose in its glory,
Signals late spring at its most elite.
Sprawling out in London's rose gardens,
A can or two as a treat.

Lighter evenings for friends,
Where we let our worries fade,
In parks with picnic spreads,
And secrets whispered as if in sin.
At sun dappled pub gardens,
Yapping about the grapevine,
Humanity and the cozzie liv cries.

Sundays by the riverside,
Lovers holding hands for the day.
Hiking through the heath,
As if it isn't a recurring treat.
Roasts are going steady,
(So, let's meet at the local?)
But barbecues are at the ready,
(I'll grab an instant coal tray-
Meet you at the park in twenty).

Backpackers 2: Social Bees

We surround ourselves with people,

    Call it being social.

        Say we're not lonely,

            In this world that can seem so

empty.

We just want the company.

Need the company.

We could dig deeper,

    Let the tears speak louder,

        Wonder why we feel this way,

Why we're in a room

full of faces that don't see us.

Not really, not under the disguise.

The smiles and easy goodbyes.

Let's go to the beach,

Take a big crowd,

Make a lot of noise,

Drink 'til our livers are
diseased.

But, no, we're not lonely.

We just can't sit there on our own,

Taking in the ocean breeze.

We're not lonely,

We're just social bees.

Taking the nectar,

So we can all be appeased.

But no, we're not lonely,

Not us,

Not we.

Not me. It's simply a need.

Seville Orange

Seville orange is my favourite nail polish.
Seville purple my favourite streak in the sky,
Sun setting on glorious days.

The colours which embody
Frolicking & fun. The river embraces the city,
Like a loving mother's arms,
The blossom careening on top of palm trees.

The clinking of ice;
Swaying & swaying in my cocktail glass.
The zest of lime,
Brings a spark back to my eyes.

Seville's orange is my favourite kind.

What is England? If not a home.

What is England?
If not a home.

What is England
if not the feeling of belonging,
that I get after a long time
abroad.

What is England
if not the mix of sand, stones & a biting sea,
which brings me peace.

What is England
if not the carefully carved meat,
crisp potatoes, honey roasted veg I feast on…

What is England
if not the Heinz baked beans,
in which I stir chilli flakes, ground cumin & fresh
spring onions.

What is England
if not the apples from my gran's garden tree,
which she'd sprinkle a dash of salt & black pepper.

What is England
if not the endless neighbourhoods of people who'd
come together at the striking of loss and grief.

What is England
if not the tutting over delayed public transport,
impatience ingrained in our psyche.

What is England
if not for steadfast friends,
who share their family's traditions with open arms.

What is England
if not celebrating every holiday,
coming together with loved ones, making memories.

What is England
if not for sparklers to celebrate Diwali,
tea lights to guide the way, ladoo and pakoras
to gift others.

What is England
if not for the people who cook in our restaurants,
Those who tend to our wounds and deliver our
takeaways.

What is England
if not for the curry houses and kebab shops after a
night out. The pizza place and local Chinese.

Fish and chips, delicious battered sausages in every city.

What is England
if not the country that brought together paprika,
cumin, turmeric, basil, black pepper, cloves,
nutmeg, coriander, vanilla, rosemary, ginger, jerk,
chilli, sumac, saffron…

…what is England if not the country
with diverse big cities,
allowing me a taste of the world and cultures
nestled into our streets.

What is England
if not the country that raised me-
in its parks, schools, university. The country I work
hard for, the land I take care of.

What is England
if not the country that gave me my dreams,
despite being the first-generation British child of
immigrants.

What is England
if it's not where I belong?

What is England if not my home?

Lemons & Limes

Sharpness bursts in my mouth
As I grin wide and free,
The yellow zest, green skins.
Eyes scrunched from the zing.

Now that we're old-ish,
And sort of free,
That lemon slice is
perfectly paired,
With my favourite bev.

It loves me,
The juniper berry.

It softens those parts of me,
Hardened from nights of grief.

What a relief,
To believe
That the citrus
Will set me free.

But it loves me,
The juniper berry.

Will it ever let me leave?

Window Seat

I'll take the window seat, thank you.
See the clouds pass by,
The Dolomites.

Eyes wide with wonder,
At skies full of thunder,
How daybreak brings with it,
A mourning-

of what's left behind;
The pine trees,
And chalky cliffs,
The way the sun glints,
Off skyscraper windows-

I'll take the window seat, thank you.
See the stars collect wishes,
As I traverse the Milky Way.

Heart full of hope,
About what the future might hold.

Let's Go Dancing

Let's go dancing in the rain.
In the onslaught of an outpour.
Dancing, until the hurt seeps away,
Gripping each other ever so tight.

Let's dive into waterfalls,
Run through valleys.
Dancing, in the glimmering sun,
Fingers clasped against the waves.

Let's take the wheel, accelerate,
Towering gum trees in the rearview.
Dancing, in the Australian heat,
Our souls sighing with relief.

Let's go dancing.

Part 2

The Pit

Note:

It's the absolute fucking pits. I hope you have people in your life who'll keep showing up until you feel whole again.

Hues of Grief

Empty. Do you see it in me?
The way your company repulses me.
Every kind word out of your mouth,
Slicing open my heart.

Shut up.

I have to do this, again?

Sometimes the fear creeps in,
That I'll have to do this, again.
Because losing you was the pits.

Can I get through it another time?
Will the next loss bring an onslaught
Of memories with you, etched forever,
On pages and pages,
My handwriting getting faster,
Pages splotched with teardrops.

Then it happens again.
And I think of airplanes in the
Morning sky, of old tales told
About travels and a life well lived.
And it's the sinking mind sand,
Of who's next.

Note To Self

What you're telling me,
Is you're one of a kind,
Dimples out, eyes unclouded.
That you're on the grind,
No worries in sight.

But honey let me tell you this,
While you push back your streaks of grey,
Sweeten your lips with Angostura Bitters,
In your egg-white cocktails,
Worries anchored in.

There's an abyss between your poised words,
And the games you play with yourself.

A fantasy of your own imagining.

Enough

I wake to the pace of life,
a video reel on fast forward

Wonder if this security
I built myself

A facade. Am I enough
Without your words

Is it right without your belief
In me

To continue and build
This life of daydreams.

I can't stop
Thinking of your smile.

I was enough for you,
And for me, for a while.

Empty

My wit has been waning,
While I've been thinking of all the things
I could have done,
differently.

My will to greet the day,
As you did, with a smile,
is shattering.

My legs ache for hours of ambling,
beside you, as you told your tales,
Of grilling freshwater fish,
The mouth-punch of pili pili,
Stopping for roadside mogo chips.

My heart is on full HD display,
As it has always been,
but without you, I am empty.

Salty

I'm feeling salty;
The punch of tears,
Leaving tracks along my cheeks,
Pool by my ears,
I lie horizontal.

I'm feeling salty;
The ice sharp mouthful of the sea,
Choking me, I gasp for air,
Eyes scanning the horizon,
Awaiting the next tumultuous wave.

I'm feeling salty;
My mum's pickled lemons,
Sharp & tangy,
Paired perfectly with warm roti,
A dark June evening outside.

I'm feeling salty;
The blood oozing from my lip,
Sharpened teeth gnawing,
I sit in this blanket of misery,
Hope- a distant friend.

I'm feeling salty;
I know the trajectory,
Of the love you promise me,
Built on whimsical moments,
Pretending you'll never leave.

I'm feeling salty;
Abandoning my mask,
Letting the truth flow free,
Allowing myself to grieve,
And let myself be.

Together (without you)

To do it (without you) is a life lived in the unknown
Not to have your shoulder to lean on,
Laughter to bathe in,
Stories to share while the morning light beckons
Streets to explore while the evening sun caresses the
crevices of pavement slabs.

To do it (without you) is a life half lived.
The chipped white paint of boats,
Roughened by the sea, soft and (without you) picked
free by me,
The gritty sand in my clothes, as I-
The clink of glass on glass, as we-
Keep unflinching eye contact,
And the beat of my heart
As I fall apart

When I wake and you're no longer alive.

Ma

The air holds whispers of your voice,
The sunset feels like the warmth,
That would rush through me when you smiled…
burning into my skin with memories
of you by the patio door,
Eyelids closed,
In a sunbeam embrace.

The way you'd place a steady hand on my back
When I engulfed you with my arms.

The streets hold secrets from our walks,
Our arms looped,
Whispering in ears about passers-by,
Asking me about my day,

Teaching me how to be kind.

Watching you pick vegetables
With as much care as when you cooked.

Apple trees are forever a core memory.

You will always be in my present,
Because not a day goes by without the sunrise
and sunset,
And it marks our very last conversation.

I think of you when the light hits the trees and leaves
a certain way.

I think of you when little birds chirp nearby;
you were the hand that'd feed them every day.

I think of you when I see hard boiled sweets;
your smile of delight would light up my life.

There's not a day that's gone by

Anniversaries

Sometimes, there's a voice,
and it wants to be heard.

To scream and shout,
pound it out.
It needs to be heard,
so very loud.

It's inside,
deep down.
That little voice,
it wants a hand to hold,
the first one it ever held.

That voice, it wants a reply
From the very man who taught it words.

That voice, it never speaks out loud.
It's just there, waiting,
waiting for me to let it out.

Just once,
it says.
Only once.
Maybe twice.
Just this month.

Then the little voice,
it lets out a sigh,
so I can tuck it up real tight,
until next time.

Cricket: Bat & Ball

Synonymous with you:
Green playing fields,
Peeling white paint from sight screens,
Varnished wooden stumps,
Stitched leather cherry-red cricket balls,
Hurtling through the air.

Synonymous with you:
Khaki green of trousers,
Loose-fitting Tusker shirts,
Evenings spent outdoors,
The knocking-in of cricket bats,
Before my brother's match wins.

I miss you, Dad.

You'll Grow Through This – Part 1

You'll grow through it,
They say

You'll be okay,
They say

Chin up,
They say

He would be proud,
They say

He's in your heart,
They say

You're strong,
They say

You're brave,
They say

You'll toughen up,
They say.

But I want to say,

I am made of memories
I am a daughter, still

You'll Grow Through This – Part 2

I see the empty fields
I glance the abandoned bat & ball.
I sieve through the vignette of memories,
I hear the faint words of praise,

But I'll never know.

I enter new seasons,
I am okay,
My chin is held level
And my heart is always full.
The strength comes in waves,

But I am soft,
I say,

And that is okay.
I am a daughter, still.

I Think You'd Be Proud

I think you'd be proud.
And that makes me smile.

Dad.

I think you'd love to hear my travel stories,
Nights camping under the glittering sky,
Eating baked beans from tins,
Spaghetti cooked in pans over campfires.

I think you'd love to hear my travel stories,
And the upsides would make you laugh;
Whales crashing in waters of New South Wales,
Thinking they were waves smashing against rocks.
Jellyfish scattered on untouched sand banks,
Mistaking them for littered empty soy sauce bottles.

And the bad shit would make you rage:
Teetering near the edges of cliff tops;
Racing on foreign roads to beat national curfews;
Chasing boys lacking emotional depth,
Instead of running through waterfalls alone.

Dad.

I think you'd love to hear my travel stories,
Meet the friends who gave me their homes,
The love I take and spread so freely,
About finding hope when I feel alone.

Dad.

I think you'd read my words,
And swell with pride,
At how far I've come.

I think you'd see how I show up,
In this world of ours;
a falcon in its prime.

Recordings

And if I had your voice
to listen to on my walks,
and if I'd thought of the loss
and if I knew,
I could've guessed
what I would want years on.

I would've recorded you.
Your voice,
your face.
The way you looked at me
and spoke so carefully.

The lilt in your voice,
the chasm in my chest,
when I realised-

-I forgot,
Or no,
I haven't forgotten

The memory of you
A clouded sky with glints of sun;

Your quirks
they're still clear as day,
your lopsided grin.
But your voice-

it escapes me.

I squeeze my eyes real tight,
Try to remember how it sounded
when you said my name.
Told me off,
taught me to read and write.

And yet,
your voice escapes me.

I wish I'd known then,
that I'd want more
than a still image,
than a sketch.

I'd want your jokes,
the mannerisms,
the lopsided smile,
the muted Kenyan in your accent.

I'd want the glint of recognition in your eyes,
When you saw your dimples in my cheeks.
I'd want your words,
The validation and praise,
The love that is so far out of my grasp.

I'd want.

1000-piece Set

Seconds pass by, Minutes vanish, Hours whiled
away, Days blend, Weeks, Years.
Wish you were still here
Obviously-

Life is a jigsaw,
And the pieces hardly fit,
But it's okay,
Because I have you to guide the way.
I'll imagine you,
Grinning, watching my rookie mistake
for choosing the 1000-piece set.

When I feel like I'm losing my marbles,
I'll smile this time and say,
*"It's okay, I have my Dad's marble set,
tucked away somewhere safe."*

Fabric

Your laughter was deep and rich,
Thick with Texan cigars,
Mingling with your aftershave.
Your tales wild, whimsical,
and off the cuff.

Travel runs in the blood it seems,
And I'll hold onto that one cut,
Of fabric that connects us,
On my adventures.

Catching flights is an
Activity for eternity.

There's no time to sleep.

I'll Meet You

I'll meet you where the sea kisses the sand,
Ride along with you down the riverside,
Walk by you on the canal path,
And catch you winking from the stream.

I'll meet you at every body of water,
Because that's where your soul resides.

I'll meet you now that you're free,
We'll go wherever you desire.

Part 3

Hope

Note:

Hope. Can we? Let's hope. Please.

Peace

Working towards peace-by-peace has felt like
unhinged behaviour.
Craving normality in a world of fatalities:
The hope of anyone who once had the will to do
more than survive.
To live a life that's dipped
into the magic powder of
Hope.

Strive for a place that is middle-ground melody,
The tune a summation of playground freedom,
And fantastical illusion. The harmony-
Includes a chorus of life's repetitive errands.
And in the mundane, let's find that peace,
In the craze, let's find that peace,
By peace in the gift of time,
Let's find peace, within ourselves…
from time to time,

let us be okay with the middle-ground melodies.

The Things We Don't Say

It's in the things we don't say.

We say,
There's a 'for sale' sign
I don't say,
Let's tear it down

But you know my heart broke to see it.
It's in the things we don't say.

We say,
It's been a while,
I don't say,
Everything is different

But you know my world is changing.
It's in the things we don't say.

We say,
The weather's so nice today,
I don't say,
I'm starving for conversation

But you know I'm trying.
It's in the things we don't say.

We say,
I love you always

I don't say,
Please don't die

But you know I'd like you around.
It's in the things we don't say.

We say,
You look beautiful,
I don't say,
It's your soul I mean

But you know I want to see you rise.
It's in the things we don't say.

We say,
Let's get an early night,
I don't say,
I can't wait for you to hold me tight

But you know my heart beats faster.
It's in the things we don't say.

We say,
I'm doing good,
I don't say,
I feel alive with something fierce

But you know.

Shades of Blue

In the shades of blue
There are you,
My joy.

In the cerulean sky
The bluish black of obsidian nights,
My joy.

In the turquoise chaos of oceans
Meeting the teal-coated tips of my nails,
My joy.

In the shades of blue,
I have found you,
You there,
Are joy.

Very Happy

I am clawing my way out of the wreckage
   Of loss.
Dismantling my fears,
While you sit and postulate
   And figure
I'm the inspiration.

Did you figure it out,
That I am not here for clout?

I am inspired and I want to inspire
But if it is the life I live
That you admire,
Then please redirect your energy
To that of my strength
Because it is far more covetable
Than the mountains I climb,
   In reality.
Focus on the mountain peaks figuratively
And there you have the beauty,

Of how I could possibly be, so very happy.

Time is a Treat

Time is endless,
Time is free.
Time is sure and a treat,
It's an everlasting escape.

Time is a gift sound in its claim,
Time will help shed your cloak of pain.
Time is a certainty riddled in uncertainty,
Time is a burden full of shame.

Time is a healer and a friend indeed,
Time is a wish come true for many.
Time is for you to use,
and abuse,
Time is endless and a dream.

Time is precious, so use it
as you please.

What's Your Fierce?

You're Fierce, you.
You with your head held high and low.
Your shoulders back,
Drooping forward over your chest
You're a fighter, aren't you?
How else could you deal with the passing storms?
Did you feel the ferocity of your strength when you
needed it?

Or is your Fierce the small and powerful voice that
told you to get on with your day?

They're both the same, in their own ways.
We see it in your eyes and the way you talk the talk.
We see it in your gait,
The way you carry yourself throughout the day.
The fear for the things that matter to you, the worry
that nobody cares.
We see it when you smile,
Eyes squinting and mouth lifting.

We know your Fierce can purr and roar all the same.

It Matters

It matters.
What you think
What you say
What you do.
It matters.

It matters.
How you show up
How you love
How you care.
It matters.

It matters.
Who you love to be near
Who you see everyday
Who you confide in.
It matters.

It matters.
Where you live
Where you traverse
Where you feel at peace
It matters.

It matters.

Better Myself

In the margins
Of life,
I'll better myself

In the corners of grief
Of quiet mornings,
I'll better myself

In the finite hours
Of time's construct,
I'll better myself

In the sluicing of waves
Of earth's freedom,
I'll better myself

In the chaos
Of our beautiful lives,
I'll better myself

I can no longer berate myself.

Darling

Darling,
Speak the sweet words to me.

Hold my hand for eternity.

Press your cheek to mine.

Touch the curves of my waist.

Darling,
Cry into my shoulder.

Caress the dimples in my cheeks.

Save your special smile for me.

Dance with me to our favourite beats.

Darling,
Love me with something fierce.

Be my darling.

My Love

Thinking of the good times,
Just me and you

Thinking of the hard times,
Just me and you,

Thinking of the best times,
You and I

Thinking of the worst of times,
You and I

Thinking of the days that pass,
My love

Thinking of the life we live,
And we love

Thinking of the down times,
Arms wrapped around

Thinking of the kind times
A kiss on my cheek

Thinking of the good times
Our whole life

My love. It's me.

Dear Change,

Are you for real this time?
You evade me.

Will you stick around? - Let me free.
Let's try this for a while. Stick around.
You find me when I lose my smile.

Change,
Are you my friend?
You seem to come when I most need you.

Change,
Are you here to hurt me?
You inflict a lot of pain to free me.

You're a constant always by my side,
I guess you're my most trying companion.

Change,
You are the reason I keep growing,
Emotionally you know no bounds.

When I ask you if I'll be alright,
You show me exactly how.

Is this forever, ever?

The fleeting impermanence of you,

in this life of uncertainties,

Makes my mistrust rise in me,

Tidal waves churn in the

belly, where the chaos I make,

From kitchen tops and my thoughts,

somersaults us onto a path,

That is right, for me. Is it? Right?

The excitement of land undiscovered,

Mushrooms hidden under shrubs,

Starfish sunbathing behind rocks

faces covered from the sun on a day,

Any day full of shrieks of delights as you hold close,

those people to you, hold tight, and close.

Want to never let go. Promise you, I'll never leave.

But the impermanence – it's attuned to you, your
fears, your desires.
And it says, with a roar, that it'll do as it pleases.

Promises are still made, and kept, and broken.
But is this forever, ever?
This path we're on, the one layered in cobbles,
pebbles, chunks of
mud, grit, the softest grass, like memory foam.

It matters?
It doesn't matter. Not this time.
Whether we choose one way
Or another.
As long as it's with good intentions,
Your whole life awaits.

Now stop wondering and never stop wandering.

Seasons of Grief, of me

I am seasoned.
In this grief of mine.
Unique,
To me.

I love cooking,
Stories about how those I've lost,
Loved me so wholly.

I am sauteed in air miles and departure lounges,
When I need space to breathe.
In writing poetry seated at corner coffee tables,
When I've tired of pushing *them* to the corners, margins,
nods, acknowledgements, and shrugs. I write-

Blending my truths,
& memories of them, far from forgotten;
my family tree, ready for picking...

I am seasoned,
Feet firm, ready,
In the only way I know how.

Wisdom

you're my reckless rock
my sandy stone
my pretty pebble
(nabbed from the beach)

when the clock hands struck distress,
the chirp of the cuckoo askew,
I held onto you

my wisdom

so sure,
invincible,
you are me-
wise and moving,
through the grief

My Golden Hues

Nice & new,
Everything so fresh & unknown
Wait until the world starts to grow.
It takes on this golden hue.
Of leaves on trees & people on the streets.
Of mountains & valleys,
That go on and on,
Ready for you to grow & explore.

You were once so small & tiny,
Ever so cute.
The love of two people,
Growing in the love of many.

You were the little smiles,
Big little yawns.

Cocooned & cared for,
Making hearts swell with love,
Your eyes made me see the world as you do.

It would do me good to remember,
The safe space in my hand,
Which you clasp with so much trust,
The love that pours from you,
The ferocious hugs,
Pulling me in every direction.

Your eyes beacons of forever.
Your world is just beginning.

But my world has your faces etched
Into memory.

All of your quirks and crazy,
The confidence in telling stories,
the jokes aplenty,
Board games and park days,
The whispered secrets,
And Nando's getaways.

Summer bucket lists, video calls
Iced oat coffees, sushi picnics, forest walks,
Reading under soft bedtime lights,
Sketching and painting for hours at a time.

The golden hues of my life,
Are so deeply rich,
Because of you.

Always loving all of you,
with something fierce.

Thanks for making me yours,
Massi • Boo • Bhua • Pua

My Heart Thawing

Don't you love the way the sun peeks through?

The grey, the misery, the defeat,
And there it is, clouds parting,
Sky lightening,
The brown bricks warming,
My heart is thawing.

Pause

To be here, must I forget you?
To be free, shrug off my grief?

But you're in every glimpse of joy.
The way raindrops cling to petals,
And how people hum along to tunes.
The hands holding, fingers interlaced,
Arms around waists.

You're in every glimpse of joy.
The way golden specks of sunlight
Kiss my skin with fervour.

Let's Talk About My Heart Sleeves

Let's talk about my heart,
It's a sweet old thing.
And its love is so cringe,
I try hard to keep it all within.

Let's talk about my heart,
And how it has a mind of its own.
When I want to fade away,
It makes me brave.

Let's talk about my heart,
Because it grieves and grieves,
For a life that's passed,
Do you know what I mean?

Let's talk about my heart,
Why is seeks for others,
To feel seen and heard,
When in doubt.

Let's talk about my heart,

Now that it's losing itself.
Is it abandoning me,
In the overgrowth?

Let's talk about my heart,
Because it grieves and grieves,
Letting me believe this is all
A joke.

Let's talk about my heart,
When it keeps beating for me,
On every starlit night,
And cloudless day.

Let's talk about my heart,
How it sits on my sleeve,
Wearing thin,
Can you believe?

To Be Alive

Drenched in perfume,
Coated in sunscreen,
Nails glistening red as if dipped in pummelled strawberries,
Lightness cloaking shoulders,
Laughter escaping lips,
Lilac and purple puncturing the sky,
As voices travel down the riverside.

Skinned knees and blackberry stains,
The crunch and pop of juicy green grapes,
Sizzling sausages on the grate,
Sliced apples sprinkled with salt & pepper.
Cherry Drops and Werther's Originals.
Learning the ABCs in Hindi.

As the melody of the past seeps into memories,
At every milestone a flicker of the past,
Climbing trees and making pillow forts.

Every new daydream,
A pause.
To be.
So very still in the here & now.

To be alive.

Chaos is Technicolour

My chaos is technicolour,

And it unravels in rivulets:

Of bruised words on pages

Of laughter in the ochre air

Of sapphire raindrops on skin

Of kisses on reddish cheeks

Of the missing peace.

Laughter Is An Antidote

You didn't even know you were healing me,
did you?

To not know me before-
the abandon with which I lived life.

Did you know you were seeing me through it?

Traversing this gaping hole in my life,
Where boundless love used to pour in
And then there was nothing. Plugged
Away, no more love to breathe in
From a woman so strong
Her every word landed as gospel.

Did you know that I was somebody different?
With fewer worries. Different worries.
That I would catch flights,
and not think of the consequences.
Someone living with abandon-

Until they were abandoned.
By the beautiful woman who gave endless hugs,
Her sharp words always sweetened for me.

Did you know you were seeing me through it?
Taking my mind away from the empty days,
which I used to fill with her presence.
Or the trips away,
Her honey gold voice through the speaker,
and my inner turmoil would cease to exist.

Did you know I was someone so different?
Who would rise to any challenge,
a voice much more decisive,
Boundaries in abundance. Sometimes.

Did you know you were seeing me-
through the endless grief,
The heaviness carried quietly in my heart.
You didn't know, did you?

But do you now know that I am someone renewed?
That there is life in my life, a softness in my heart,
a hardness still at times, but I no longer grieve,

The same.

Did you know that because of you,
I learnt to love this world again,
And find the joys in all the moments,
And memories made with you.

Now you know.

I want to be in love

I want to be in love with this life,
My early mornings,
And late nights.

I want to be in love with this life,
My voice being recognised,
At the end of the phone line.

I want to be in love with this life,
The rough brush of grass against my bare feet,
When I visit my family.

I want to be in love with this life,
Passing of time collapsing,
After years between meeting.

I want to be in love with this life,
Dancing in the rain,
At every opportunity.

Acknowledgements

I'm grateful to those who offered their critique on the poetry within these pages, and for doing so with such kindness. Writing fiction and sharing it is hard; it forces you to consider how others might perceive you through your words. But writing the poems in this collection has felt like something else entirely: soul-baring on a page. Believe it or not, I've kept a lot to myself, but I am excited to share these words with you, my readers, and I hope that at the very least, you're inspired to book flights and catch feelings.

I've been unapologetically myself here. My love for those I've lost, the stories of travelling through Vietnam, Thailand, Australia—honestly, everywhere I've experienced—are all here, spliced throughout different poems. So, to those who offered critiques that helped me improve the poems, thank you for handling my words with care.

Thanks to Ryan Norman for your detailed feedback. Kay Burrows, Khyati Sanger, and Monti Rodgers - I am ever grateful for how graciously you accepted my request for a read-through, feedback, and the tightest, most ambitious deadline. And thank you to my creative writing groups for always being such keen readers and generous supporters of all my work. And Hazel — I know we haven't been sounding boards for this project, for once, but thank you for being a part of my book writing journey: I am surely a stronger storyteller because of our never-ending back and forth.

A very special shoutout to my friend and the ever-talented Claire Addicott. We both know that *I want to be in love with this life*, and so it goes that I am in love with the cover design. Thank you for humouring my creative direction (which was, at times, questionable) and for truly seeing these poems at their essence, then turning them into something visually stunning – I am so in love with your art.

I could not have done this without my friends being so very accommodating to my spontaneous *(forced?)* requests (Niall, I'll exchange cooking for a proofread any day). Kara — how are you still reading my words at this point? You deserve a break from my non-stop questions at all hours of the day and night. You're an absolute diamond.

To my closest go-to friends – I love your endless encouragement, motivation, and understanding. Please, *let's go dancing in the rain (and in the Australian heat)*.

Danielle – this collection wouldn't have come together if not for your belief in my first-draft magic of every poem I've ever written. Many of my favourite *memories are made with you.*

The people I love are scattered throughout these pages. I hope you catch glimpses of yourselves in the memories; please know that I love you immeasurably.

About the author

Originally from London, Arti is an avid traveller with a deep appreciation for cultures and cuisines. She has authored two books, including the thought-provoking short story about social media, *His Side, Her Side, Facebook & The Truth,* and the perfect escapist beach read, *The Beauty of Decisions.*

Seasons of Grief is her debut poetry collection.

With expertise in Italy and Australia, Arti's writing reflects her extensive global experiences. She brings over a decade of experience in writing and content communication within the travel and lifestyle publishing industry, along with a career in academic and book publishing.

Come @ Me

Socials: @CLCLTravel

Food & travel platform:
www.citylivingcoastalloving.com

Books: www.artirajput.com

Printed in Dunstable, United Kingdom